Estelle M. Hurll

Jean Francois Millet

Estelle M. Hurll

Jean Francois Millet

1st Edition | ISBN: 978-3-75236-140-7

Place of Publication: Frankfurt am Main, Germany

Year of Publication: 2020

Outlook Verlag GmbH, Germany.

Reproduction of the original.

JEAN FRANÇOIS MILLET

BY
ESTELLE M. HURLL

INTRODUCTION

I. ON MILLET'S CHARACTER AS AN ARTIST

The distinctive features of Millet's art are so marked that the most inexperienced observer easily identifies his work. As a painter of rustic subjects, he is unlike any other artists who have entered the same field, even those who have taken his own themes. We get at the heart of the matter when we say that Millet derived his art directly from nature. "If I could only do what I like," he said, "I would paint nothing that was not the result of an impression directly received from nature, whether in landscape or in figure." His pictures are convincing evidence that he acted upon this theory. They have a peculiar quality of genuineness beside which all other rustic art seems forced and artificial.

The human side of life touched him most deeply, and in many of his earlier pictures, landscape was secondary. Gradually he grew into the larger conception of a perfect harmony between man and his environment. Henceforth landscape ceased to be a mere setting or background in a figure picture, and became an organic part of the composition. As a critic once wrote of the Shepherdess, "the earth and sky, the scene and the actors, all answer one another, all hold together, belong together." The description applies equally well to many other pictures and particularly to the Angelus, the Sower, and the Gleaners. In all these, landscape and figure are interdependent, fitting together in a perfect unity.

As a painter of landscapes, Millet mastered a wide range of the effects of changing light during different hours of the day. The mists of early morning in Filling the Water-Bottles; the glare of noonday in the Gleaners; the sunset glow in the Angelus and the Shepherdess; the sombre twilight of the Sower; and the glimmering lamplight of the Woman Sewing, each found perfect interpretation. Though showing himself capable of representing powerfully the more violent aspects of nature, he preferred as a rule the normal and quiet.

In figure painting Millet sought neither grace nor beauty, but expression. That he regarded neither of these first two qualities as intrinsically unworthy, we may infer from the grace of the Sower, and the naïve beauty of the Shepherdess and the Woman Sewing. But that expression was of paramount interest to him we see clearly in the Angelus and the Man with the Hoe. The leading characteristic of his art is strength, and he distrusted the ordinary elements of prettiness as taking something from the total effect he wished to produce. "Let no one think that they can force me to prettify my types," he said. "I would rather do nothing than express myself feebly."

It was always his first aim to make his people look as if they belonged to their station. The "mute inglorious Milton" and Maud Muller with her "nameless longings" had no place on his canvases. His was the genuine peasant of field and farm, no imaginary denizen of the poets' Arcady. "The beautiful is the fitting," was his final summary of æsthetic theory, and the theory was put into practice on every canvas.

In point of composition Millet's pictures have great excellence. "I try not to have things look as if chance brought them together," he said, "but as if they had a necessary bond between them." So nothing is accidental, but every object, however small, is an indispensable part of the whole scheme.

An important characteristic of his work is its power to suggest the third dimension of space. The figures have a solid, tangible appearance, as if actually alive. The Gleaners, the Woman Churning, and the Man with the Hoe are thoroughly convincing in their reality.

The picture of the Gleaners especially has that so-called "quality of circumambient light" which circulates about the objects, so to speak, and gives them position in space. Millet's landscapes also have a depth of spaciousness which reaches into infinite distance. The principles of composition are applied in perspective as well as laterally. We can look into the picture, through it, and beyond it, as if we were standing in the presence of nature.

Mr. Bernhard Berenson goes so far as to say that this art of "space composition," as he terms it, can "directly communicate religious emotion," and explains on this ground the devotional influence of Perugino's works, which show so remarkable a feeling for space.[1] If he is right, it is on this principle, rather than because of its subject, that the Angelus is, as it has sometimes been called, "one of the greatest religious paintings of the age."

While Millet's art is, in its entirety, quite unique, there are certain interesting points of resemblance between his work and that of some older masters. He is akin to Rembrandt both in his indifference to beauty and in his intense love of human nature. Millet's indifference to beauty is the more remarkable because in this he stood alone in his day and generation, while in the northern art of the seventeenth century, of which Rembrandt is an exponent, beauty was never supreme.

As a lover of human nature, Millet's sympathies, though no less intense than Rembrandt's, were less catholic. His range of observation was limited to peasant life, while the Dutch master painted all classes and conditions of men. Yet both alike were profound students of character and regarded expression as the chief element of beauty. Rembrandt, however, sought expression principally in the countenance, and Millet had a fuller understanding of the expressiveness of the entire body. The work of each thus complements that of the other.

Millet's passion for figure expression was first worked out in painting the nude. When he abandoned such subjects for the homelier themes of labor, he gave no less attention to the study of form and attitude. The simple clothing of the peasant is cut so loosely as to give entire freedom of motion to the body, and it is worn so long that it shapes itself perfectly to the figure. The body thus clad is scarcely inferior to the nude in assuming the fine lines of an expressive pose.

Millet's instinct for pose was that of a sculptor. Many of the figures for his pictures were first carefully modelled in wax or clay. Transferred to canvas they are drawn in the strong simple outlines of a statue. It is no extravagant flight of fancy which has likened him to Michelangelo. In the strength and seriousness of his conceptions, the bold sweep of his lines, and, above all, in the impression of motion which he conveys, he has much in common with the great Italian master. Like Michelangelo, Millet gives first preference to the dramatic moment when action is imminent. The Sower is in the act of casting the seed into the ground, as David is in the act of stretching his sling. As we look, we seem to see the hand complete its motion. So also the Gleaners, the Women Filling the Water-Bottles, and the Potato Planters are all portrayed in attitudes of performance.

When Millet represents repose it is as an interval of suspended action, not as the end of completed work. The Shepherdess pauses but a moment in her walk and will immediately move on again. The man and woman of the Angelus rest only for the prayer and then resume their work. The Man with the Hoe snatches but a brief respite from his labors. The impression of power suggested by his figure, even in immobility, recalls Michelangelo's Jeremiah.

To the qualities which are reminiscent of Michelangelo Millet adds another in which he is allied to the Greeks. This is his tendency towards generalization. It is the typical rather than the individual which he strives to present. "My dream," he once wrote, "is to characterize the type." So his figures, like those of Greek sculpture, reproduce no particular model, but are the general type deduced from the study of many individuals.

[1]

4

II. ON BOOKS OF REFERENCE

Since the death of Millet, in 1875, much that is interesting and valuable has been written of his life and work. The first biography of the painter was that by his friend Sensier, in a large illustrated volume whose contents have been made familiar to English readers by an abridged translation published in this country simultaneously with the issue of the French edition. Containing all the essential facts of Millet's outward life, besides a great number of the artist's letters, together with his autobiographical reminiscences of childhood, Sensier's work is the principal source of information, from which all later writers draw. Yet it is not an altogether fair and satisfactory presentation of Millet's life. Undue emphasis is laid upon his struggles with poverty, and the book leaves much to be desired.

Julia Cartwright's recent work, "Jean François Millet: His Life and Letters," is founded on Sensier's life, yet rounds out the study of the master's character and work with the fuller knowledge with which family and friends have described his career.

Another recent book called "J.F. Millet and Rustic Art" is by Henry Naegely (published in England), and is critical rather than biographical in purport. It is a sympathetic appreciation of Millet's art and character, and grows out of a careful study of the painter's works and an intimate connection with the Millet family.

Besides these books devoted exclusively to the subject, the life work of Millet is admirably sketched in brief form in the following more general works:—

Richard Muther's "History of Modern Painting," Mrs. Stranahan's "History of French Painting," Rose G. Kingsley's "History of French Art," and D.C. Thomson's "Barbizon School."

Of great importance to the student of Millet are the various articles contributed to the magazines by those who knew and understood the painter. The following are of special note: By Edward W. Wheelwright, in "The Atlantic Monthly," September, 1876; by Wyatt Eaton, in the "Century," May, 1889; by T.H. Bartlett, in "Scribner's," May and June, 1890; by Pierre Millet, in "Century," January, 1893, and April, 1894; and by Will Low, in "McClure's," May, 1896. Julia Cartwright, in the preface to the above mentioned biography, mentions other magazine articles not so generally accessible.

III. HISTORICAL DIRECTORY OF THE PICTURES OF THIS COLLECTION

Portrait frontispiece, a life-size crayon made by Millet in 1847 and given to his friend Charlier. It afterwards became the property of Sensier.

1. *Going to Work*, one of several versions of the subject in different mediums, oil, pastel, drawing, and etching. This picture was painted in 1851, and was at one time (1891) in a private collection in Glasgow.[1] It is to be distinguished from the picture of 1850, where the woman carries a pitcher instead of a rope. [2]

2. *The Knitting Lesson*, a drawing corresponding in general composition, with some changes of detail, to the small painting (17 by 14-1/2 in.) of the subject in the collection of Mrs. Martin Brimmer, in the Museum of Fine Arts, Boston.

3. *The Potato Planters*, painted in 1862, and exhibited at the great exhibition at Paris of that year, also again in 1867 at the International Exhibition. It changed hands for large sums during the painter's lifetime, and is now in the Quincy A. Shaw collection, Boston, Mass.

4. *The Woman Sewing by Lamplight*, painted in 1872, and sold in 1873 for 38,500 francs, the highest price at that time ever paid for one of Millet's works.

5. *The Shepherdess*, painted in 1862, and exhibited at the Salon of 1864, also again at the Exposition Universelle of 1867. It is now in the collection of M. Chauchard.

6. *The Woman Feeding Hens*, a charcoal sketch, corresponding in general composition to the description of a painting bearing the same name, which was painted in 1854 for M. Letrône for 2000 francs.

7. *The Angelus*, an oil painting measuring 25 by 21 in. The first drawing for the picture was sold February, 1858. The painting was completed for exhibition in the Salon of 1859. It was declined by the patron for whom it was intended, and finally sold to a Belgian artist in 1860, and soon afterwards to the Belgian minister. The original price was 2000 francs. The picture passed from one owner to another, and in 1873 was bought by J.W. Wilson for 50,000 francs, later bringing at the Wilson sale of 1881 the sum of £6400. In

an auction sale of the Secrétan collection, July, 1889, there was an immense excitement over the contest between the French government, represented by M. Proust, Director of Fine Arts, and various American dealers, who were determined to win the prize. It was finally knocked down to M. Proust for 553,000 francs, but the French government refused to ratify the purchase, and the picture was brought to the United States. Here the customs duty exacted was so enormous (£7000) that the picture remained only six months (the duty being waived during that period), and after being exhibited throughout the country finally returned to France, where it was purchased for £32,000 by M. Chauchard, who has the finest collection of Millets in existence.

8. *Filling the Water-Bottles*, a charcoal drawing, which attracted much attention when exhibited in the Millet collection of the Paris Exposition, 1889.

9. *Feeding Her Birds*, painted in 1860, and exhibited in Salon of 1861. Presented by a purchaser to the Museum of Lille in 1871.

10. *The Church at Gréville*, sketched during Millet's visit at Gréville in the summer of 1871; referred to by him, in a letter of 1872, as still in process of painting; found in his studio at the time of his death, in 1875. The picture was bought by the French government, and is now in the Louvre, Paris.

11. *The Sower*, the second painting of the subject, painted in 1850, and exhibited in the Salon of 1850-51. It is now in the Vanderbilt collection, New York.

A pencil sketch of the Sower is in the collection of Millet's drawings, at the Boston Museum of Fine Arts.[3]

12. *The Gleaners*, a painting first exhibited at the Salon of 1867. It was sold to M. Binder of l'Isle Adam for 2000 francs. In 1889 it was purchased by Madame Pommeroy for 300,000 francs, and presented to the Louvre, Paris. A pencil drawing of the three figures is in the collection of the Boston Museum of Fine Arts.

13. *The Milkmaid*, painted in 1871 from a sketch made in Gréville. Seen in Millet's studio in 1873 by Will Low, the American artist.

14. *The Woman Churning*, one of several versions of the subject, the first of which appeared in 1870.

15. *The Man with the Hoe*, painted in 1862 and exhibited at the Salon of 1863. Sold to a Belgian collector, and long in Brussels. It is now owned by Mr. W.S. Crocker of San Francisco, Cal.

[1]

    See D.C. Thomson's *Barbizon School*, pp. 226, 227.

[2]

    See Julia Cartwright, *Life and Letters of Jean François Millet*, pp. 114,115.

[3]

    This is one of an interesting collection of drawings in this museum, which also contains several original paintings by Millet, a Shepherdess, seated, a portrait of the painter, and others. Other fine Millets are in the private collections of Boston, where the painter received early appreciation, owing to the enthusiasm of William Morris Hunt, the painter, and such connoisseurs as Mr. Quincy Shaw and Mr. Brimmer.

IV. OUTLINE TABLE OF THE PRINCIPAL EVENTS IN MILLET'S LIFE

1814.	• Millet born, October 4, in hamlet of Gruchy, commune of Gréville, in the old province of Normandy, France.
1832.	• Two months' study with Mouchel in Cherbourg. • Death of Millet's father. • Study with Langlois in Cherbourg.
1837.	• Removal to Paris, supported by annuity of 400 francs from the municipality of Cherbourg.[1]
1837-1839 (?).	• Studies with Delaroche.[2]
1840.	• A portrait of M.L.F. exhibited at Salon of the Louvre.
1841.	• Portrait of Mademoiselle Antoinette Feuardent. • Marriage with Mademoiselle Pauline Virginie Ono in Cherbourg.

1842.
- Returned to Paris.

1844.
- Millet exhibited at Salon: the Milkmaid, the Riding Lesson.
- Death of Millet's wife, April 21, and Millet's return home for 18 months.

1845.
- Marriage with Catherine Lemaire late in summer, in Gréville.
- Visit in Havre in November.
- Arrival in Paris in December, and residence in the rue Rochehouart.

1847.
- Oedipus taken from the Tree exhibited at the Salon.

1848.
- Millet exhibited at the Salon the Winnower, bought by M. Ledru-Rollin for 500 francs, and the Captivity of the Jews in Babylon.

1849.
- Removal to Barbizon.

1850.
- The Sower painted and exhibited at the Salon with the Sheaf Binders.

1851.
- Death of Millet's grandmother, Louise Jumelin, at Gruchy.

1853.
- Death of Millet's mother at Gruchy.
- Millet exhibited at the Salon:
  - Ruth and Boaz,   bought by an American.
  - The Sheep Shearer, bought by William Morris Hunt
  - The Shepherd,

1854.	• Visit four months to the surroundings of the old home in Normandy.

- 1855. • The Grafter, exhibited at the Salon.

- 1856. • Le Pare aux Moutons painted.

- 1857. • The Gleaners exhibited at the Salon.

- 1859. • The Angelus exhibited at the Salon.

1860-1861.	• The Shepherd in the Fold by Moonlight, and the Femme aux Seaux.

- • The Potato Planters painted.
- • Millet exhibited at the Salon of the Champs Elysèes:

1861.
  - • Feeding Her Birds.
  - • Waiting.
  - • The Sheep Shearer.

- • List of pictures painted:—

1862.
  - • Winter.
  - • The Crows.
  - • Sheep Feeding.
  - • The Wool Carder.
  - • The Stag.
  - • The Birth of the Calf.
  - • The Shepherdess.
  - • The Man with the Hoe.

1863.
- Millet sent to Salon: Man with the Hoe, The Wool Carder (see list of works in 1862), and a Shepherd bringing Home his Sheep.

1864.
- Millet exhibited at the Salon: The Shepherdess, and The Birth of the Calf (see list of works in 1862).

1865.
- Completion of decorative pictures for M. Thomas: Spring and Summer, panels 8 by 4 ft., set in the woodwork; Autumn for the ceiling; Winter for the chimneypiece.

1866.
- Short visit to Vichy, Auvergne, Clermont, Issoire.

- Millet exhibited at the Exposition Universelle (International Exhibition):—

1867.
- Death and the Woodcutter (refused by the Salon of 1859).
- The Gleaners.
- The Shepherdess.
- The Sheep Shearer.
- The Shepherd.
- The Sheep Fold.
- The Potato Planters.
- The Potato Harvest.
- The Angelus.
- Visit to Vichy in June.

1867-69.
- The Pig Killers.

1868.
- Millet made Chevalier of the Legion of Honor, August 13.
- Journey with Sensier in Alsace and Switzerland, September.

1870.
- Millet elected, March 24, juror for coming exposition.
- The Woman Churning exhibited at the Salon.

- Departure for Gréville on account of danger of remaining in Barbizon during the war.

1871.
- Return to Barbizon November 7.

1874.
- Order from Administration of Beaux Arts for mural decorations in the Panthéon (Ste. Geneviève), Paris.
- The Priory painted.

1875.
- Death of Millet, January 20, at Barbizon.

[1]

To this was added later 600 francs from the General Council of La Manche, but both annuities were soon discontinued.

[2]

The exact date of Millet's severing connection with Delaroche is not mentioned by his biographers, though the circumstances are detailed.

V. SOME OF MILLET'S ASSOCIATES

Companions in the studio of Delaroche:—
Charles François Hébert (1817-).
Jalabert (1819-).
Thomas Couture (1815-1879).
Edouard Frère (1819-1886).
Adolphe Yvon (1817-).
Antigna (1818-1878).
Prosper Louis Roux (1817-).
Marolle.
Cavalier, sculptor.
Gendron (1817-1881).

Friends and neighbors in Paris:—
Couture (also fellow student in studio of Delaroche).

Tourneaux (1809-1867), painter and poet.
Diaz (1808-1876), landscape painter.
Joseph Guichard (1836-1877), marine painter.
Charles Jacque (1813-), etcher.
Camprédon.
Séchan, clever scene painter.
Diéterle, clever scene painter.
Eugène Lacoste.
Azevédo, musical critic.

Friends at Barbizon:—

Charles Jacque (who removed thither with him).
Diaz (also a friend of the Paris days).
Corot (1796-1875).
Theodore Rousseau (1812-1867).
Laure (1806-1861).
William Morris Hunt, American painter.
Mr. Hearn, American painter.
Mr. Babcock, American painter.
Edward Wheelwright, American painter.
Wyatt Eaton, American painter.
Will Low, American painter.

I

GOING TO WORK

On the other side of the Atlantic Ocean, where the sea forms a narrow channel separating the British Isles from the European continent, lies that part of France known as the old province of Normandy. There is here a very dangerous and precipitous coast lined with granite cliffs. The villages along the sea produce a hardy race of peasants who make bold fishermen on the water and thrifty farmers on the land.

To this Norman peasant stock belonged Jean François Millet, the painter of the pictures reproduced in this little book. He was brought up to hard out-of-door labor on his father's farm in the village of Gréville, but when the artistic impulses within him could no longer be repressed, he left his home to study art. Though he became a famous painter, he always remained at heart a true peasant. He set up his home and his studio in a village called Barbizon, near the Forest of Fontainebleau, not many miles from Paris. Here he devoted all his gifts to illustrating the life of the tillers of the soil. His subjects were drawn both from his immediate surroundings and from the recollections of his youth. "Since I have never in all my life known anything but the fields," he said, "I try to say, as best I can, what I saw and felt when I worked there." It is now a quarter of a century since the painter's life work ended, and in these years some few changes have been made in the customs and costumes which Millet's pictures represented. Such changes, however, are only outward; the real life of peasant labor is always the same. Seedtime and harvest, toil, weariness and rest, the ties of home and of religion, are subjects which never grow old fashioned.

In France the farm labors are shared by men and women alike. The peasant woman is sturdily built, and her healthy out-of-door life makes her very strong. She is fitted by nature and training to work beside the men in the fields. In our first picture we see a young man and woman starting out together for the day's work.

GOING TO WORK

It is morning, and the early sun illumines the distant plain, where ploughing has already begun. The light falls on the two figures as they walk down the sloping hillside.

They are dressed for their work in clothing which is plain and coarse, but which is perfectly suited for the purpose. The French peasants' working clothes are usually of strong homespun cloth, fashioned in the simplest way, to give the wearers entire ease in motion. They are in the dull blues, browns, and reds which delight the artist's eye. Such colors grow softer and more beautiful as they fade, so that garments of this kind are none the less attractive for being old. Ragged clothing is seldom seen among peasants. They are too thrifty and self-respecting to make an untidy appearance.

The men wear soft felt hats, the brim of which can be pulled forward to shade the eyes. The women cover their heads neatly with caps or kerchiefs, and are nearly always seen with aprons. Men and women both wear the heavy wooden shoes called *sabots*, in which the feet suffer no pressure as from leather shoes, and are protected against the moisture of the ground.

The peasants of our picture carry all they need for the day's work. A three-pronged fork rests across the man's shoulder, and a wallet of lunch hangs from his left arm. The woman has a basket, a linen sack, and a bit of rope. Evidently something is to be brought home. Just now she has swung the empty basket up over her shoulders and it covers her head like a huge sunbonnet.

The two young people are full of the healthy vigor which makes work a pleasure. They go cheerfully to their day's task as if they really enjoyed it. We cannot help suspecting that they are lovers. The man carries himself erect with a conscious air of manliness, and steps briskly, with his hand thrust into his pocket. The girl hides her shyness in the shadow of the basket as she turns her face towards his. The two swing along buoyantly, keeping step as if accustomed to walking together.

At the close of the day's work the basket and sack will be filled, and the laborers will return to their home by the same way. The burden may be heavy, but they will bear it as the reward of their toil.

The picture of Going to Work was painted at about the same time[1] as the The Sower, which forms one of the later illustrations of our collection. A comparison of the pictures will show interesting points of resemblance between the two men striding down hill. Though Going to Work is not as a work of art of equal rank with The Sower, we get in both pictures a delightful sense of motion which makes the figures seem actually alive.

[1]

That is, within a year. See dates in the *Historical Directory*.

II

THE KNITTING LESSON

In the picture we have been examining we have seen something of the outdoor life of the French peasants, and now we are shown the interior of one of their houses, where a Knitting Lesson is being given. The girls of the French peasantry are taught only the plainest kinds of needlework. They have to begin to make themselves useful very early in life, and knitting is a matter of special importance. In these large families many pairs of stockings are needed, and all must be homemade. This is work which the little girls can do while the mother is busy with heavier labors. The knitting work becomes a girl's constant companion, and there are few moments when her hands are idle.

THE KNITTING LESSON

The little girl in our picture is still a beginner in the art, and the lesson is a very exciting occasion to her. Already she feels like a woman.

The mother and daughter have their chairs by the window to get a good light on the work. It is a large and beautiful casement window, of the kind almost universal in France, opening lengthwise in the middle in two parts which swing on hinges like doors. The window seat serves as a table, to hold the basket and scissors. The doll is thrust into the corner; our little girl has "put away childish things"—at least for the moment,—and takes her task very seriously.

The two chairs are drawn close together, the one a small counterpart of the other. The child braces her feet firmly on one of the rounds and bends her whole mind to her work. Both mother and daughter wear close white caps, though the little girl's is of a more childish pattern and does not cover her pretty hair in front.

The mother has been sewing on some large garment which lies across her lap. She lets the little girl work by herself for a time, and then stops to set her right. Already a considerable length of stocking has been made, but this is a place where close attention is needed. Perhaps it is time to begin shaping the heel. The mother's work is left altogether for a moment. Putting her arm about the child's shoulder, she takes the two little hands in hers, and guides the fingers holding the needles.

We get some idea of the quaint style of the building from this glimpse of the living-room. Probably it is a low stone cottage with thatched or tiled roof. The deep window seat shows how thick the walls are. Overhead we see the oak rafters.

The room looks spotlessly clean, as a good housewife's should. Though we see only a corner, that corner holds the most precious household possession, the linen chest. It stands against the wall, and is of generous size. French country people take great pride in storing up a quantity of linen; tablecloths, sheets, shirts, pillowcases, often of their own weaving, are piled in the deep clothes-presses. In well-to-do families there are enough for six months' use, the family washing taking place only twice a year, in spring and fall, like house-cleaning in America. We judge that our housekeeper is well provided, by the pile of neatly folded sheets on the press. The little clock, high on the wall, and the vase of flowers on the chest are the only touches of ornament in the room. On the wall are some small objects which look like shuttles for weaving.

As we look at the picture we feel sure that Millet was a lover of children, and it is pleasant to know that he had many of his own. The artist father was his children's favorite playmate, and at the close of his day's work in his studio, they ran to meet him with shouts of joy. He used to like to walk about the garden with them showing them the flowers. In winter time they sat together by the fire, and the father sang songs and drew pictures for the little ones. Sometimes taking a log from the wood basket he would carve a doll out of it, and paint the cheeks with vermilion. This is the sort of doll we see on the window seat in our picture.

Ruskin tells us that a true artist feels like a caged bird in painting any enclosed space, unless it contains some opening like a door or window. No amount of beauty will content us, he says, if we are shut in to that alone. Our picture is a good proof of this principle. We can easily fancy how different the effect would be without the window: the room would appear almost like a prisoner's cell. As it is, the great window suggests the out-of-door world into which it opens, and gives us a sense of larger space.

Our illustration is taken from a drawing. Millet was a painstaking artist who made many drawings and studies for his paintings. This is probably such a study, as there is also a painting by him of the same subject very similar to this.

III

THE POTATO PLANTERS

In the picture called The Potato Planters we are reminded at once of the peasants we have already seen in Going to Work. We see here married people a few years older than the young people of the other picture working together in the fields.

It may be that this is their own little plot of ground, for they work with a certain air of proprietorship. They look prosperous, too, and are somewhat better dressed than common laborers. It is the highest ambition of the French peasant to own a bit of land. He will make any sacrifice to get it, and possessing it, is well content. He labors with constant industry to make it yield well.

The field here is at quite a distance from the village where the workers live. We can see the little group of houses on the horizon. In France the agricultural classes do not build their dwelling-houses on their farms, but live instead in village communities, with the farms in the outlying districts. The custom has many advantages. The families may help one another in various ways both by joining forces and exchanging services. They may also share in common the use of church, school, and post office. This French farming system has been adopted in Canada, while in our own country we follow the English custom of building isolated farmhouses.

In working season the French farmer must go daily to his labor at a distance. The people in our picture are fortunate enough to own a donkey which is their burden-bearer between house and field. The strong little creature can carry a heavy load properly disposed in pannier baskets. The panniers are made very deep and wide, but rather flat, so as to fit the sides of the donkey. With one of these hanging on each side of the saddle, the weight of the burden is so well distributed that it is easily borne.

The donkey of our picture has been relieved of his panniers, and now rests in the shade of some apple-trees. One of the baskets is in the mean time put to a novel use. Made soft and warm with a heavy cloak, it forms a nice cradle for the baby. The babies in French peasant families are often left at home with the grandmother, while the mother goes out to field work. The painter Millet himself was in childhood the special charge of his grandmother, while his mother labored on the farm. The people of our picture have another and, as it seems, a much pleasanter plan, in going to the field as a family party.

The day is well advanced and the work goes steadily on. It is potato planting, and the potato crop is of great importance to country people, second perhaps to the wheat, as it supplies food to both man and beast. The commoner varieties, as the large white, are raised for cattle, and the finer and sweeter kinds, the red and the yellow, are kept for the table.

The laborer and his wife move along the field, facing each other on opposite sides of the row they are planting. The man turns the sod with his hoe, a short-handled tool which long practice has taught him to use skilfully. The wife carries the potato seed in her apron, and as her husband lifts each spadeful of earth, she throws the seed into the hole thus made. He holds the hoe suspended a moment while the seed drops in, and then replaces the earth over it. The two work in perfect unison, each following the other's motion with mechanical regularity, as they move down the field together.

The two who work so well together in the field are sure to work well together in the home. The man has the serious, capable look of a provident husband. The woman looks like a good housewife. That shapely hand throwing the seed so deftly into the ground is well adapted to domestic tasks.

We may easily identify our picture as a familiar scene in Millet's Barbizon surroundings. We are told that "upon all sides of Barbizon, save one, the plain

21

stretches almost literally as far as the eye can reach," and presents "a generally level and open surface." "There are no isolated farmhouses, and no stone walls, fences, or hedges, except immediately around the villages; and were it not all under cultivation, the plain might be taken for a vast common."[1]

It is evident, then, that we here see the plain of Barbizon and true Barbizon peasants of Millet's day. The villagers of the painter's acquaintance were on the whole a prosperous class, nearly all owning their houses and a few acres of ground. The big apple-tree under which the donkey rests is just such an one as grew in Millet's own little garden.

Fruit trees were his peculiar delight. He knew all their ways, and "all their special twists and turnings;" how the leaves of the apple-tree are bunched together on their twigs, and how the roots spread under ground. "Any artist," he used to say, "can go to the East and paint a palm-tree, but very few can paint an apple-tree."

[1]

From Edward Wheelwright's *Recollections of Jean François Millet*, in *Atlantic Monthly*, September, 1876.

IV

THE WOMAN SEWING BY LAMPLIGHT

Though the peasant women of France have so large a share in the laborious out-of-door work on the farms, they are not unfitted for domestic duties. In the long winter evenings they devote themselves to more distinctly woman's tasks, knitting and sewing, sometimes even spinning and weaving. Their housekeeping is very simple, for they live frugally, but they know how to make the home comfortable. Many modern inventions are still unknown to them, and we should think their customs very primitive, but on this account they are perhaps even more picturesque.

There is contentment in every line of the face of this Woman Sewing by Lamplight. It is the face of a happy young wife and mother. She sits close by her baby's bedside that she may listen to his gentle breathing as he sleeps, and she smiles softly to herself while she sews. It is a sweet face which bends over the work, and it is framed in the daintiest of white caps edged with a wide ruffle which is turned back over the hair above the forehead, that it may not shade her eyes.

The garment that lies on her lap is of some coarse heavy material. No dainty bit of fancy work is this, but a plain piece of mending. It may be the long cloak which the shepherd wraps about him in cold and stormy weather. Made from the wool grown on his own sheep, spun by his wife's own hand, it is unrivalled among manufactured cloths for warmth and comfort. The needle is threaded with a coarse thread of wool, which the sewer draws deftly through the cloth.

On a pole which runs from floor to ceiling is a hook, from which a lamp is suspended by a chain. This lamp appears to be a boat-shaped vessel with the wick coming out at one end. The light gilds the mother's gentle profile with shining radiance; it illumines the fingers of her right hand, and gleams on the coarse garment in her lap, transforming it into a cloth of gold.

The baby meanwhile lies on the other side of the lamp in the shadow. His little mouth is open, and he is fast asleep. We can almost fancy that the mother croons a lullaby as she sews. There is a pathetic little French song called La Petite Hélène, which Millet's mother used to sing to him, and which he in turn taught his own children. Perhaps we could not understand the words if we could hear it. But when mothers sing to their babies, whatever the tongue in which they speak, they use a common language of motherhood. Some such simple little lullaby as this, which mothers of another land sing to their babes, would doubtless interpret this mother's thoughts:—

"Sleep, baby, sleep!
Thy father watches the sheep;
Thy mother is shaking the dreamland tree,
And down comes a little dream on thee.
Sleep, baby, sleep!

"Sleep, baby, sleep!
The large stars are the sheep;
The little ones are the lambs, I guess:
The gentle moon is the shepherdess,
Sleep, baby, sleep!

"Sleep, baby, sleep!
Our Saviour loves his sheep;
He is the Lamb of God on high
Who for our sakes came down to die.
Sleep, baby, sleep!"

When we remember that the ancient Romans had lamps constructed somewhat like that in the picture, it seems strange that so rude a contrivance should be in use in the nineteenth century. But this is only the practical and prosaic side of the question. For artistic purposes the lamp is just what is wanted in the composition.

You can see how a lamp with a glass chimney and shade would spoil the whole effect. We should lose that strange beautiful halo surrounding the wick, and the light would fall only on the work, instead of glorifying the face of the mother. These wonderful impressions of light add much to the artistic beauty of the picture, and explain why artists have so greatly admired it.

The picture naturally recalls that other Mother and Babe, Mary of Nazareth and the holy Child Jesus, who for so many centuries have inspired the imagination of artists. Often a painter has drawn his first conception for this sacred subject from some peasant mother and child such as these.

In order to give religious significance to their pictures, artists have tried in many ways to suggest the supernatural. They have introduced halos about the heads of Mary and Jesus, and have made the light seem to shine mysteriously from the child's body. Now our painter Millet, representing only an ordinary mother and babe, has not used any such methods. Nevertheless, without going beyond strict reality, he has produced a mystical effect of light which makes this picture worthy of a place among the Madonnas. The glow of the lamp transforms the familiar scene into a shrine of mother's love.

V

THE SHEPHERDESS

Many years ago the early English poet, Sir Philip Sidney, wrote a book about an imaginary country called Arcadia, noted for the sweetness of the air and the gentle manners of the people. As he described the beauties of the scenery there, he told of "meadows enamelled with all sorts of eye-pleasing flowers; each pasture stored with sheep feeding with sober security; here a shepherd's boy piping as though he should never be old; there a young shepherdess knitting and withal singing, and it seemed that her voice comforted her hands to work, and her hands kept time to her voice-music."

We could easily fancy that our picture of the Shepherdess was meant to illustrate a scene in Arcadia. Here is the meadow "enamelled with eye-pleasing flowers," the sheep "feeding with sober security," and the young shepherdess herself knitting. Though she is not singing with her lips, her heart sings softly as she knits, and her hands keep time to the dream-music.

Early in the morning she led her flock out to the fallow pastures which make good grazing ground. All day long the sheep have nibbled the green herbage at their own sweet will, always under the watchful eye of their gentle guardian. Her hands have been busy all the time. Like patient Griselda in Chaucer's poem, who did her spinning while she watched her sheep, "she would not have been idle till she slept." Ever since she learned at her mother's knee those early lessons in knitting, she has kept the needles flying. She can knit perfectly well now while she follows her flock about. The work almost knits itself while her eyes and thoughts are engaged in other occupations.

The little shepherdess has an assistant too, who shares the responsibilities of her task. He is a small black dog, "patient and full of importance and grand in the pride of his instinct."[1] When a sheep is tempted by an enticing bit of green in the distance to stray from its companions, the dog quickly bounds after the runaway and drives it back to the flock. Only the voice of the shepherdess is needed to send him hither, thither, and yon on such errands.

Now nightfall comes, and it is time to lead the flock home to the sheepfold. The sheep are gathered into a compact mass, the ram in their midst. The shepherdess leads the way, and the dog remains at the rear, "walking from side to side with a lordly air," to allow no wanderer to escape.

THE SHEPHERDESS

Their way lies across the plain whose level stretch is unbroken by fences or buildings. In the distance men may be seen loading a wagon with hay. The sheep still keep on nibbling as they go, and their progress is slow. The shepherdess takes time to stop and rest now and then, propping her staff in front of her while she picks up a stitch dropped in her knitting. There is a sense of perfect stillness in the air, that calm silence of the fields, which Millet once said was the gayest thing he knew in nature.

The chill of nightfall is beginning to be felt, and the shepherdess wears a hood and cape. Her face shows her to be a dreamer. These long days in the open air give her many visions to dream of. Her companionship with dumb creatures makes her more thoughtful, perhaps, than many girls of her age.

As a good shepherdess she knows her sheep well enough to call them all by name. From their soft wool was woven her warm cape and hood, and there is a genuine friendship between flock and mistress. When she goes before them, they follow her, for they know her voice.

Among the traditions dear to the hearts of the French people is one of a saintly young shepherdess of Nanterre, known as Ste. Geneviève. Like the shepherdess of our picture, she was a dreamer, and her strange visions and wonderful sanctity set her apart from childhood for a great destiny. She grew up to be the saviour of Paris, and to-day her name is honored in a fine church

28

dedicated to her memory. It was the crowning honor of Millet's life that he was commissioned to paint on the walls of this church scenes from the life of Ste. Geneviève. He did not live to do the work, but one cannot help believing that his ideals of the maiden of Nanterre must have taken some such shape as this picture of the Shepherdess.

In the painting from which our illustration is reproduced, the colors are rich and glowing. The girl's dress is blue and her cap a bright red. The light shining on her cloak turns it a rich golden brown. Earth and sky are glorified by the beautiful sunset light.

As we look across the plain, the earth seems to stretch away on every side into infinite distance. We are carried out of ourselves into the boundless liberty of God's great world. "The still small voice of the level twilight" speaks to us out of the "calm and luminous distance."

Ruskin has sought to explain the strange attractive power which luminous space has for us. "There is one thing that it has, or suggests," he says, "which no other object of sight suggests in equal degree, and that is,—Infinity. It is of all visible things the least material, the least finite, the farthest withdrawn from the earth prison-house, the most typical of the nature of God, the most suggestive of the glory of his dwelling place."[2]

[1]

Like the watchdog described in Longfellow's *Evangeline*, Part II.

[2]

In *Modern Painters*, in chapter on "Infinity," from which also the other quotations are drawn.

VI

THE WOMAN FEEDING HENS

In walking through a French village, we get as little idea of the home life of the people as if we were in a large town or city. The houses usually border directly upon the street, and the spaces between are closed with high walls, shutting in the thoroughfare as completely as in a city "block." Behind these barriers each family carries on its domestic affairs in the privacy of its own domain. The *cour*, or dooryard, is the enclosure adjoining the house, and is surrounded on all sides by buildings or walls. Beyond this the more prosperous have also a garden or orchard, likewise surrounded by high walls.

In the dooryard are performed many of the duties both of the barn and the house. Here the cows are milked, the horses groomed, the sheep sheared, and the poultry fed. Here, too, is the children's playground, safe from the dangers of the street, and within hearing of the mother's voice.

It is into such a dooryard that we seem to be looking in this picture of The Woman Feeding Hens. It is a common enough little house which we see, built of stone, plastered over, in the fashion of the French provinces, and very low. In the long wall from the door to the garden gate is only one small high window. But time and nature have done much to beautify the spot. In the cracks of the roof, thatched or tiled, whichever it may be, many a vagrant seed has found lodgment. The weeds have grown up in profusion to cover the bare little place with leaf and flower. Indeed, there is here a genuine roof garden of the prettiest sort, and it extends along the stone wall separating the dooryard from the garden. Some one who has seen these vine-fringed walls in Barbizon describes them as gay with "purple orris, stonecrop, and pellitory."

A young wife presides in the little cottage home and rules her side of the dooryard with gentle sway. She has a curly-haired baby boy who creeps after

31

her as she goes about her work. His inquiring mind is at this age investigating all the corners of the house, and before long he will be the young master of the dooryard.

The housewife boasts a small brood of hens. Early in the morning the voice of the chanticleer is heard greeting the dawn. Presently he leads his family forth to begin their day's scratching in the dooryard. Here and there they wander with contented clucks, as they find now and then a worm or grub for a titbit. But it is only a poor living which is to be earned by scratching. The thrifty housewife sees to it that her brood are well fed. At regular times she comes out of the house to feed them with grain, as she is doing now.

The baby hears the mother's voice saying, in what is the French equivalent, "Here chick-chick-chick," and creeps swiftly to the door. He, too, tries to call "chick-chick." He watches the odd creatures eagerly as they gobble up the seed. They stand about in a circle, heads all together in the centre, bobbing up and down as long as any food remains. Chanticleer holds back with true gallantry, and with an air of masculine superiority. The belated members of the brood come running up as fast as they can. The apron holds a generous supply, so that there is enough for all, but the housewife doles it out prudently by the handful, that none may suffer through the greediness of the others.

As we study the lines of the picture a little, they teach us some important lessons in composition. We note first the series of perpendicular lines at regular intervals across the width of the picture. These counterbalance the effect of the long perspective which is so skilfully indicated in the drawing of the house and the garden walk. The perspective is secured chiefly by three converging lines, the roof and ground lines of the house, and the line of the garden walk. These lines if extended would meet at a single point.

Once more let us recall Ruskin's teaching in regard to enclosed spaces.[1] The artist is unhappy if shut in by impenetrable barriers. There must always be, he says, some way of escape, it matters not by how narrow a path, so that the imagination may have its liberty.

This is the principle which our painter has applied in his picture. He wisely gives us a glimpse of the sky above, and shows us the shady vista of the garden walk leading to the great world beyond.

Our illustration is from a charcoal drawing, which, like the Knitting Lesson, is matched by a corresponding painting.

[1]

In *Modern Painters* in the chapter on "Infinity."

VII

THE ANGELUS

The early twilight of autumn has overtaken two peasants at the close of a day's work in the field. They are gathering the potato harvest. The dried plants are first pulled up, and the potatoes carefully dug out of the holes. Then the vegetables are taken from the furrows by the basketful, and poured into brown linen sacks to be carried home on the wheelbarrow. One of these sacks is not yet quite full, and the work has been prolonged after sunset.

The field is a long way from the village, but in the still air sounds are carried far across the plain. Suddenly the bell of the village church peals forth. The man stops digging and plunges his fork into the earth, and the woman hastily rises from her stooping posture. The Angelus bell is ringing, and it calls them to prayer.

Three times each day, at sunrise, midday, and sunset, this bell reminds the world of the birth of Jesus Christ. The strokes are rung in three groups, corresponding to the three parts of The Angelus, which are recited in turn. The first word gives the bell its name,—Angelus, the Latin for angel.

"The angel of the Lord announced to Mary,
And she conceived of the Holy Spirit.

"Behold the handmaid of the Lord,
Be it done unto me according to thy word.

"And the word was made flesh
And dwelt among us."

Thus run the words of the translation in the three couplets into which they are separated, and then this prayer is added: "We beseech thee, O Lord, pour forth thy grace into our hearts; that as we have known the incarnation of thy Son Jesus Christ by the message of an angel, so by his cross and passion we may be brought into the glory of his resurrection, through the same Jesus Christ our Lord."

Besides this, after each couplet of the Angelus, is recited that short hymn of praise, beginning with the words which the angel of the annunciation addressed to Mary,[1] "Ave Maria." This is why the hour after sunset is so often called the hour of Ave Maria. The English poet Byron has written of this solemn moment:—

"Ave Maria! blessed be the hour!
The time, the clime, the spot, where I so oft
Have felt that moment in its fullest power
Sink o'er the earth so beautiful and soft,
While swung the deep bell in the distant tower,
Or the faint dying day-hymn stole aloft,
And not a breath crept through the rosy air,
And yet the forest leaves seemed stirred with prayer."

THE ANGELUS

The atmosphere of prayer pervades the picture. The woman stands with bowed head and hands clasped over her breast. Her whole body sways slightly forward in the intensity of her devotion. Her husband has bared his head and holds his hat before him. Though he may seem somewhat awkward, he is not less sincerely reverent.

The sunset light shines on the woman's blue apron, gilds the potato sacks in the wheelbarrow, and gleams along the furrows. Farther away, the withered plants are heaped in rows of little piles. Beyond, the level plain stretches to meet the glowing sky, and, outlined on the horizon, is the spire of the church where the bells are ringing.

As the meaning of the picture grows upon us, we can almost hear the ringing of the bells. Indeed, to those familiar with such scenes in actual life, the impression is very vivid. The friend to whom Millet first showed his painting immediately exclaimed, "It is the Angelus." "Then you can hear the bells," said the artist, and was content.

The solemn influence of the picture is deepened by the effects of the twilight on the plains. A wide outlook across a level country, like a view of the sea, is always impressive, but it has peculiar power in the vague light which follows the sunset. Many poetic natures have felt this mystic spell of the gloaming as it descends upon the plain. Robert Louis Stevenson was one of these, and upon visiting Barbizon he described vividly his feelings at such an hour. We are told also that Millet loved to walk abroad at nightfall and note the mysterious effects of the twilight. "It is astonishing," he once said to his brother in such a walk, "how grand everything on the plain appears, towards the approach of night, especially when we see the figures thrown out against the sky. Then they look like giants."

In nearly all of Millet's pictures people are busy doing something. Either hands or feet, and sometimes both hands and feet, are in motion. They are pictures of action. In the Angelus, however, people are resting from labor; it is a picture of repose. The busy hands cease their work a moment, and the spirit rises in prayer. We have already seen, in other pictures, how labor may be lightened by love. Here we see labor glorified by piety.

The painting of the Angelus has had a remarkable history. The patron for whom it was first intended was disappointed with the picture when finished, and Millet had no little difficulty in finding a purchaser. In the course of time it became one of the most popular works of the painter, and is probably better known in our country than any other of his pictures. In 1889 it was bought by an American, and was carried on an exhibition tour through most of the large cities of the United States. Finally it returned to France, where it is now in the collection of M. Chauchard.

The Angelus is one of the few of Millet's works which have changed with time. The color has grown dark and the canvas has cracked somewhat, owing to the use of bitumen in the painting.

[1]

    "Hail Mary"; see St. Luke, chapter i., verse 28.

VIII

FILLING THE WATER-BOTTLES

The artist Millet loved to draw as well as to paint. Black and white pictures had their charm for him as truly as those in color. Indeed, he once said that "tone," which is the most important part of color, can be perfectly expressed in black and white. It is therefore not strange that he made many drawings. Some of these, like the Knitting Lesson and the Woman Feeding Hens, were, as we have seen, studies for paintings. The picture called Filling the Water-Bottles was, on the other hand, a charcoal drawing, corresponding to no similar painting. It is in itself a finished work of art.

It is a typical French river scene which we see here, and it gives us an idea how large a part a river may take in the life of French country people. Sometimes it is the sole source of water for a village. Then it is not only the common village laundry, in which all clothing is washed, but it is also the great village fountain, from which all drinking-water is drawn.

The women in our picture have come to the bank with big earthen jars to fill. It is in the cool of early morning, and the mist still lies thick over the marshes bordering the river. The sun, seen through the mist, looks like a round ball. On the farther bank, where a group of poplars grow, some horsemen ride up to ford the stream. They, too, are setting forth early on their day's work. One is already half across.

The women have picked out, along the marshy bank, a point of land jutting into the river like a miniature promontory, and seemingly of firm soil. It is only large enough to hold one at a time, so they take turns. One is now filling a bottle, while the other waits, standing beside two jars.

The first woman kneels on the ground, and supporting herself firmly by placing one hand on the edge of the bank, she grasps the jar by the handle, with her free right hand, and swings it well out over the water. Experience has taught her the most scientific way of filling the jar with least muscular strain. She does not try to plunge it down into the water, but holding it on its side, slightly tipped, draws it along with the mouth half under the surface, sucking in the water as it moves. We see what hard, firm muscles she has to hold the arm out so tensely. Her arm acts like a compass describing the arc of a circle through the water with the jar. As we look, we can almost see her completing the circle, and drawing up the full jar upon the bank.

The woman who waits her turn is capable of the same feat. There is power in every line of her figure as she stands in what has been well described by a critic as a "majestic pose." She straightens back to rest, with her arms on her hips, quite unconscious that there is anything fine in her appearance.

Look a minute and you will see that she is the woman of the Angelus. As we saw her in the other picture, with head bowed and hands clasped on her breast, we did not realize how grand and strong she was. But raising her head, throwing back her chest, and putting her arms on her sides, she shows us now her full power.

Both women are dressed alike in the clothing which is now familiar to us from the other pictures,—coarse gowns made with scanty skirts, long aprons reaching nearly to the bottom of the dress, kerchiefs fastened snugly about their heads, and wooden sabots. We could not imagine anything that would become them better. It is part of the French nature to understand the art of dressing, and this art is found just as truly among the peasants of the provinces as in the fashionable world at Paris.

The picture is a study in black and white which any one who cares for drawing will wish to examine attentively. He was indeed a master who could, with a single bit of charcoal, make us feel the witchery of this early morning hour by the river-side. We note the many different "tones" of the picture,—the faint soft mist of the distant atmosphere over the marshes, growing darker on the poplars and the hilly bank in the middle distance; the shadow of the bank in the river; the gleam of the sunlight on the calm water mid-stream; the ripples about the jar; the sharply defined figures of the women, dark on the side turned from the sun; and the quivering shadow of the kneeling woman in the ripple-broken water in front.

Among primitive peoples the hour of sunrise was a sacred time, when hymns were sung and sacrifices were offered to the life-giving sun. The painter Millet has expressed something of the mystic solemnity of the hour in this picture. The sun has awakened the world to work, and in its strength men and women go forth to labor.[1]

[1]

A fine passage on the morning occurs in Thoreau's second chapter of *Walden*.

IX

FEEDING HER BIRDS

As we have already seen in the picture of the Woman Feeding Hens, the dooryard in French village homes is so shut in by walls, that it has the privacy of a family living-room. This was the arrangement in Millet's own home at Barbizon. The painter was among the fortunate ones who had a garden beyond the dooryard. At the other end of this was his studio, where he worked many hours of the day. It is said that he used to leave the door open that he might hear the children's voices at their play. Sometimes, indeed, he would call them in to look at his pictures, and was always much pleased when they seemed to understand and like them. We may be sure that he often looked across the garden to the dooryard where the family life was going on, and at such times he must have caught many a pretty picture. Perhaps our picture of this mother feeding her children was suggested in this way.

Three healthy, happy children have been playing about in the yard,—a girl of six, her younger sister, and a brother still younger. They are dressed simply, so as to enjoy themselves thoroughly without fear of injuring any fine clothes. All three wear long aprons and wooden sabots. The little girls have their flying hair confined in close bonnet caps tied under the chin. The boy rejoices in a round cap ornamented on top with a button. The sisters take great care of their little brother.

The toys are of a very rude sort and evidently of home manufacture. A cart is constructed of a board set on clumsy wheels. A doll is roughly shaped of wood and wrapped in a hood and blanket. There is a basket besides, in which one can gather bits of treasure picked up here and there in the yard.

FEEDING HER BIRDS

By and by the play is interrupted by a familiar voice. The children look up and see their mother standing smiling in the doorway. A bowl which she has in her hand is still steaming, and an appetizing odor reminds them that they are hungry. The basket and the cart are hastily dropped, but not the doll, and they all run to the doorstep. The brother is placed in the middle and the sisters seat themselves on either side. The elder girl still holds her doll with maternal solicitude; the other two children clasp hands, and the sister's arm is put around the boy's neck.

Meanwhile the mother has seated herself directly in front of them, on a low stool such as is used by country people as a milking-stool. She tips it a little as she leans over to feed the children in turn from a long handled wooden spoon. Of course the first taste is for the little brother, and he stretches out his neck eagerly, opening his mouth wide so as not to lose a drop. The sisters look on eagerly, the younger one opening her own mouth a little, quite unconsciously. An inquisitive hen runs up to see what good things there are to eat. In the garden beyond, the father works busily at his spading.

The name which Millet gave to this picture is the French word *Becquée*, which cannot be translated into any corresponding word in English. It means a *beakful*, that is, the food which the mother bird holds in her beak to give to the nestlings.

The painter had in mind, you see, a nestful of birds being fed. The similarity between the family and the bird life is closely carried out in the picture. The children sit together as snugly as birds in a nest. The mother bends toward them in a brooding attitude which is like the bird mother's. Her extended hand suggests a bird's beak, tapering to a sharp point at the end of the spoon. The young bird's mouth is wide open, and in pops the nice spoonful of broth! The house itself is made to look like a cosy little nest by the vine that embowers it. The sturdy stem runs up close by the doorstep and sends out over door and window its broad branches of beautiful green leaves.

And just as the father bird watches the nest from his perch on some branch of the tree, the father at work in the garden can look from time to time at the little family circle in the doorway. As in the picture of the Woman Feeding Hens, the house is built of stone covered with plaster. The door casing is of large ill-matched blocks of stone. The dooryard is made to appear much larger by the glimpse of the orchard we get through the gateway. No out-of-door picture is complete which does not show something of the beauty of nature. The dooryard itself would be a bare place but for the shady garden beyond.

X

THE CHURCH AT GRÉVILLE

The village-commune of Gréville has nothing to make it famous except that it was the birthplace of the painter Millet. It is at the tip of Cape La Hague, which juts abruptly from the French coast into the English channel. The cape is a steep headland bristling with granite rocks and needles, and very desolate seen from the sea. Inland it is pleasant and fruitful, with apple orchards and green meadows.

The village life centres about the church, for the inhabitants of Grenville are a serious and God-fearing people. The church is the spot around which cluster the most sacred associations of life. Here the babies are baptized, and the youths and maidens confirmed; here the young people are married, and from here young and old alike are carried to their last resting-place. The building is hallowed by the memories of many generations of pious ancestors.

The Millet family lived in an outlying hamlet (Gruchy) of Grenville, and were somewhat far from the church. Yet they had even more associations with it than other village families. Here our painter's father had early shown his talent for music at the head of the choir of boys who sang at the Sunday service. Here at one time his old uncle priest, Charles Millet, held the office of vicar and went every morning to say mass.

Among the earliest recollections of Jean François was a visit to the church of Gréville at a time when some new bells had just been bought. They were first to be baptized, as was the custom, before being hung in the tower, and it was while they still stood on the ground that the mother brought her little boy to see them. "I well remember how much I was impressed," he afterwards said, "at finding myself in so vast a place as the church, which seemed even more immense than our barn, and how the beauty of the big windows, with their lozenge-shaped panes, struck my imagination."

At the age of twelve the boy went to be confirmed at the church of Gréville, and thenceforth had another memorable experience to associate with the place. The vicar, who questioned him, found him so intelligent that he offered to teach him Latin. The lessons led to the poems of Virgil, which opened a new world to him.

THE CHURCH AT GRENVILLE

Years passed; the boy became a man and the man became a famous artist. But the path to fame had been a toilsome one, and as Millet pressed on his way he was able to return but seldom to the spots he had loved in his youth, and then only on sad errands. At length the time came (1871) when the artist brought his entire family to his native Grenville to spend a long summer holiday. Millet made many sketches of familiar scenes which gave him material for work for the next three years. One of these pictures was that of the village church, which he began to paint sitting at one of the windows of the inn where the family were staying.

If the building had lost the grandeur it possessed for his childish imagination, it was still full of artistic possibilities for a beautiful picture.

It is a solid structure, and we fancy that the builders did not have far to bring the stone of which it is composed. The great granite cliffs which rise from the sea must be an inexhaustible quarry. The building is low and broad, to withstand the bleak winds. A less substantial structure, perched on this plateau, would be swept over the cliffs into the sea. There is something about it suggestive of the sturdy character of the Norman peasants themselves, strong, patient, and enduring. It is very old; the passing years have covered the walls with moss, and nature seems to have made the place her own. It is as if, instead of being built with hands, it were a portion of the old cliffs themselves.

The grassy hillock against which the church nestles is filled with graves, a cross here and there marking the place where some more important personage is buried. Here is the sacred spot where Millet's saintly old grandmother was laid to rest. A rough stone wall surrounds the churchyard, as old and moss-grown as the building itself. Some stone steps leading into the yard are hollowed by the feet of many generations of worshippers. In the rear is a low stone house embowered in trees.

The square bell-tower lifts a weather-vane against the sky, and the birds flock about it as about an old home. The rather steep roof is slightly depressed, as if beginning to sink in.

With a painter's instinct Millet chose the point of view from which all the lines of the church would be most beautiful and whence we may see to the best advantage the quaint outlines of the tower. Beside this, he took for his work the day and hour when that great artist, the sun, could lend most effective help. So we see the simple little building at its best. The sky makes a glorious background, with fleecy clouds delicately veiling its brilliancy. The bright light throws a shadow of the tower across the roof, breaking the monotony of its length. The bareness of the big barn-like end is softened by the shadow in which it is seen. The plain side is decorated with the shadows of the buttresses and window embrasures.

The sheep are as much at home here as the birds. They nibble contentedly in the road by the wall, and are undisturbed by the approach of a villager. Beyond, at the left, is a glimpse of the level stretch of the sea. This is a spot where earth and sky and water meet, where the fishermen from the sea and the ploughmen from the fields come to worship God.

XI

THE SOWER

It is nightfall, and the sky is cloudy save where the last rays of the setting sun illumine a spot on the horizon. While the light lasts, the Sower still holds to his task of sowing the seed. A large sack of grain is fastened about his body and hangs at his left side, where one end of it is grasped firmly in the left hand lest any of the precious seed be spilled. Into this bag he plunges his right hand from time to time, and draws out a handful of grain which he flings into the furrow as he walks along.

The Sower's task ended, a series of strange transformations begins in the life of the seed. The winter rain softens and swells it, and when spring comes it pushes its way up in a tiny shoot. Soon the slender blades appear in close lines; by and by the stalks grow tall and strong, and the field is full of the beautiful green grain.

THE SOWER

Then the hot summer sun shines with ripening power; the wheat turns a golden yellow; the ears bend under the weight of the grain, and it is time for the harvest. The reapers come with sickle and scythe, and the grain is cut, and bound into great sheaves. The thrashing follows, when the ear is shaken off the stalk, and the grain is winnowed. And now the mills take up the work, the golden wheat grains are crushed, and the fine white flour which they contain is sifted and put into bags. The flour is mixed and kneaded and baked, and at length comes forth from the oven a fragrant loaf of bread.

Now bread is a necessity of life to the people, and the supply of bread turns on the history of the seed. If the harvest is plenty, the people may eat and be happy. If it is poor, they suffer the miseries of hunger. If it fails altogether, they die of starvation. It is then a solemn moment when the seed is planted. Often the sower begins his task by tossing a handful of grain into the air in the sign of a cross, offering a prayer for a blessing on the seed. His is a grave responsibility; every handful of seed means many loaves of bread for hungry mouths. He must choose the right kind of seed for his soil, the right kind of weather for the planting, and use the grain neither too lavishly nor too sparingly.[1]

This is why the Sower in our picture takes his task so seriously. He carries in his hand the key to prosperity. He is a true king. Peasant though he is, he feels the dignity of his calling, and bears himself royally. He advances with a long swinging stride, measuring his steps rhythmically as if beating time to inaudible music. His right arm moves to and fro, swinging from the shoulder as on a pivot, and describing the arc of a circle.

The hilly field in which he works is such as the painter Millet was familiar with in his peasant childhood in Normandy. A yoke of oxen are drawing the plough in the distance, as is the custom in that province. The Sower himself is a true Norman peasant.

It is interesting to trace the outlines of the composition. There is first the long line on the Sower's right side, beginning at the shoulder and following the outer edge of the right leg to the ground. On the other side, curving to meet this, is a line which begins at the top of the head, follows the left arm and the overhanging sack, and is faintly continued by the tiny stream of seed which leaks from the corner of the bag and falls near the Sower's foot. Crossing these curves in the opposite direction are the lines of the right arm and the left leg. Thus the figure is painted in strong simple outlines such as we see in the statues by great sculptors.

The line defining the edge of the field against the sky, sloping in the direction in which the Sower walks, adds to the impression of motion which is so strongly suggested by the picture. As we look, we almost expect to see the

Sower reach the foot of the slope, and stride out of sight, still flinging the grain as he goes.

There is another thing to note about the composition, and that is the perfect proportion of the single figure to the canvas which it so completely fills. This was the result of the painter's experiments. In the haste of his first inspiration he did not allow space enough to surround the Sower.[2] He then carefully traced the figure on a larger canvas and made a second picture. Afterwards the same subject was repeated in a Barbizon landscape.

Our American poet William Cullen Bryant has written a poem called "The Song of the Sower," which is very suggestive in connection with Millet's painting.[3] This is the way the song ends:—

"Brethren, the sower's task is done,
The seed is in its winter bed.
Now let the dark-brown mould be spread,
To hide it from the sun,
And leave it to the kindly care
Of the still earth and brooding air,
As when the mother, from her breast,
Lays the hushed babe apart to rest,
And shades its eyes, and waits to see
How sweet its waking smile will be.
The tempest now may smite, the sleet
All night on the drowned furrow beat,
And winds that, from the cloudy hold,
Of winter breathe the bitter cold,
Stiffen to stone the yellow mould,
   Yet safe shall lie the wheat;
Till, out of heaven's unmeasured blue
Shall walk again the genial year,
To wake with warmth and nurse with dew
The germs we lay to slumber here."

[1]

For farmer's lore as to the diverse soils and diverse planting seasons, see Virgil's *Eclogues*, books i. and ii.

[2]

In spite of this imperfection the first Sower is a highly prized painting and is in the Quincy-Shaw Collection, Boston.

[3]

Compare also Victor Hugo's poem, often referred to in descriptions of this picture, *Saison des Semailles: Le Soir.*

XII

THE GLEANERS

It is harvest time on a large farm. The broad fields have been shorn of their golden grain, and men and women are still busy gathering it in. The binders have tied the wheat in sheaves with withes, the sheaves are piled upon a wagon and carried to a place near the farm buildings, where they are stacked in great mounds resembling enormous soup tureens. The overseer rides to and fro on his horse giving orders to the laborers.

Now come the gleaners into the field to claim the time-honored privilege of gathering up the scattered ears still lying on the ground. The custom dates back to very early times.[1] The ancient Hebrews had a strict religious law in regard to it: "When ye reap the harvest of your land, thou shalt not make clean riddance of the corners of thy field when thou reapest, neither shalt thou gather any gleaning of thy harvest: thou shalt leave them unto the poor, and to the stranger."[2] Another law says that the gleanings are "for the fatherless and for the widow; that the Lord thy God may bless thee in all the work of thine hands."[3]

This generous practice is still observed in France. The owner of a grain field would be afraid of bad luck to the harvest if he should refuse to let the gleaners in after the reapers. Gleaning is, however, allowed only in broad daylight, that no dishonest persons may carry away entire sheaves.

It is near noon of a summer day, and the sun is high in the heavens, casting only small shadows about the feet. The gleaners are three women of the poorer peasant class. They are tidily dressed in their coarse working clothes, and wear kerchiefs tied over their heads, with the edge projecting a little over the forehead to shade the eyes. The dresses are cut rather low in the neck, for theirs is warm work.

They make their way through the coarse stubble, as sharp as needles, gathering here and there a stray ear of the precious wheat. Already they have collected enough to make several little bundles, tied neatly, and piled together on the ground at one side.

THE GLEANERS

As we look at them closely we see that they represent the three ages of womanhood: there is a maiden, a matron, and an old woman. The nearest figure, standing at the right, is the eldest of the three. She cannot bear the strain of stooping long at a time, and bends stiffly and painfully to her task. Next her is a solidly built woman, with square figure and a broad back capable of bearing heavy burdens. Those strong large hands have done hard work. The third figure is that of a young woman with a lithe, girlish form. With a girl's thought for appearance she has pinned her kerchief so that the ends at the back form a little cape to shield her neck from the burning sun. Unlike her companions, she wears no apron. While the others use their aprons doubled up to form sacks for their gleanings, she holds her grain in her hand.

If you will try in turn each one of the positions taken by the several figures, you will see how differently the three work. The two who put the grain in the apron, or pass it into the hand which rests on the knee, must every time lift themselves up with an awkward backward motion. The younger gleaner has found a short and direct route from one hand to the other, by resting the left hand, palm up, upon the back, where the right can reach it by a simple upward motion of the arm which requires no exertion of the body. Her method saves the strength and is more graceful.

Moving forward in the stooping posture, with eyes fixed upon the ground, the figures of the gleaners have been compared to great grasshoppers, making their odd, irregular, hopping progress across the field. Even as we look they seem to move toward us.

The picture is a fine study in lines. The middle figure is constructed in a square outline, and this square effect is emphasized in various ways,—by the right angle formed between the line across the bust and the right arm, by the square corner between chin and neck, and by the square shape of the kerchief at the back of the head. We thus get an idea of the solid, prosaic character of the woman herself.

The younger woman is a creature of beautiful curves. The lines of her back and bust flow together in an oval figure which the position of the left arm completes. The outstretched right arm continues the fine line across the back. The lovely curve of the throat, the shapeliness of the hand, even the pretty adjustment of the kerchief, lend added touches to the charm of the youthful figure.

The lines of the standing figure curve towards the other two, and carry the composition to sufficient height. The lines enclosing the entire group form a mound-like figure not unlike a wheat stack in shape. A wheat stack faintly seen across the distance in the centre of the field marks the apex of the mound, the sides being formed by the outer lines of the two outer figures.

When we compare the picture with the others we have seen in the same general style of composition, showing a level plain with figures in front, we note how much more detail the background of the Gleaners contains. This is because the figures do not come above the horizon line, as do those in the Angelus and Shepherdess. Hence the eye must be led upward by minor objects, to take in the entire panorama spread before us.

[1]

See the Book of Ruth.

[2]

Leviticus, chapter xxiii., verse 22.

[3]

Deuteronomy, chapter xxiv., verse 19.

XIII

THE MILKMAID[1]

All through the years of Millet's life and work in Barbizon, his thoughts used to turn often to the little village in Normandy where he spent his youth. His early life in the fields impressed upon his memory all the out-of-door sights peculiar to his native province. The customs of peasants in France differ in the various provinces just as do ours in the various states. Some of the household utensils in Millet's childhood's home were such as he never saw elsewhere, and always remembered with pleasure. The ways of doing the work in Gréville were not altogether like the ways of Barbizon, and Millet's observant eye and retentive memory noted these differences with interest. When he revisited his home in later life, he made careful sketches of some of the jugs and kitchen utensils used in the family. He even carried off to his Barbizon studio one particular brass jar which was used when the girl went to the field to milk cows. He also sketched a girl carrying a jug of milk on her shoulder in the fashion of the place. Out of such studies was made our picture of the Milkmaid. "Women in my country carry jars of milk in that way," said the painter when explaining the picture to a visitor at his studio, and went on to tell of other features of the life in Normandy, which he reproduced in his pictures, though some of them he had not seen in all the long time since his boyhood. As a reminiscence of Normandy the Milkmaid is a companion piece to the Sower. There are other points of resemblance between the two pictures, as we shall see.

THE MILKMAID

The day draws to its close in splendor, and the western sky is all aflame. Against this brilliant background the figure of the Milkmaid looms up grandly as she advances along the path through the meadow. She is returning from the field which lies on the other slope of the hill. There the cows are pastured and a rude fence marks the boundary. The girl has been out for the milking, and a cow near the fence turns its head in the direction of her retreating figure.

The milk is carried in a large jar on the left shoulder. By holding the left arm akimbo, hand resting on the hip, the girl makes her shoulder a little broader, as it were, enlarging the support of the jar. The way in which the burden is kept in place is very interesting. To put up the right arm to steady it would be impossible, for the arm is not long enough to insure a firm grasp upon so heavy a weight. So a cord or strap is passed through the handle of the jar, carried over the head, and held in the right hand. The strong arm is stretched tense to keep the strap tight. The head must of course be protected from the straining of the cord, the shoulder from the pressure of the jar. Both are therefore well padded. The head pad resembles a cap hanging in lappets on each side. Even with this protection the girl's face shows the strain.

A picture like this teaches us that there are other ways of giving a figure beauty than by making the face pretty. Just as Millet's Shepherdess differs altogether from the little Bopeep of the nursery tale, so this peasant girl is not at all like the pretty milkmaids who carry milking-stools and shining pails through the pages of the picture books. Millet had no patience with such pictures. Pretty girls were not fit for hard work, he said, and he always wanted to have the people he painted look as if they belonged to their station. Fitness was in his mind one of the chief elements of beauty.

So he shows us in this Milkmaid a young woman framed in the massive proportions of an Amazon, and eminently fitted for her lot in life. Her chief beauty lies in the expression of her splendidly developed figure. Her choicest gifts are the health and virtue which most abound in the free life of God's country.

"God made the country, and man made the town.
What wonder, then, that health and virtue, gifts
That can alone make sweet the bitter draught
That life holds out to all, should most abound
And least be threatened in the fields and groves."[2]

A study of the lines of the picture will show the artistic beauty of the composition. You may trace a long beautiful curve beginning at the girl's finger tip and extending along the cord across the top of the milk jar. Starting from the same point another good line follows the arm and shoulder across the face and along the edge of the jar. At the base of the composition we find corresponding lines which may be drawn from the toe of the right foot. One follows the diagonal of the path and the other runs along the edge of the lifted skirt.

There are other fine lines in the drawing of the bodice and the folds of the skirt. Altogether they are as few in number and as strongly emphasized, though not so grand, as those of the Sower.

[1]

The title of Water-Carrier has been incorrectly attached to this picture, though the sketch on which it is based is properly known as the Milkmaid.

[2]

From Cowper's *Task*.

XIV

THE WOMAN CHURNING

Again we are in the picturesque province of Normandy, and are shown the interior of a dairy where a woman is busy churning. It is a quaint place, with raftered ceiling and stone-paved floor, and the furnishings are only such as are required by the work in hand. On some wooden shelves against the farther wall are vessels of earthenware and metal, to hold cream, cheese, butter, and the like. The churn is one of the old-fashioned upright sort, not unlike those used in early New England households, and large enough to contain a good many quarts of cream. The woman stands beside it, grasping with both hands the handle of the dasher, or plunger, which is worked up and down to keep the cream in motion and so change it into butter.

In the beginning of the churning process the movement of the dasher is slow, so that the cream may be thoroughly mixed. Then it goes more rapidly for a time, till, just as the arms grow weary, the butter begins to "come," when the speed slackens to the end, the entire process occupying thirty or forty minutes. The butter collects in yellow lumps, which are at length taken from the churn, washed and kneaded to press out the buttermilk, and then moulded into pats. The pleasure of the finishing touches makes up for the fatiguing monotony of the churning. George Eliot, in the novel of "Adam Bede," gives a charming description of Hetty Sorrel's butter-making, with all the pretty attitudes and movements of patting and rolling the sweet-scented butter into moulds.

We can hardly tell, from the attitude of the woman in our picture, how far her work has progressed, but her expression of satisfaction seems to show that the butter is "coming" well. The work of butter-making varies curiously at different times. Sometimes the butter comes quickly and easily, and again, only after long and laborious delays. There seems, indeed, no rule about the process; it appears to be all a matter of "luck." Country people have always been very superstitious in regard to it; and not understanding the true reasons for a successful or an unsuccessful churning, they attribute any remarkable effects to supernatural agencies.

In the old days of witchcraft superstitions, they used to think that when the cream did not readily turn to butter, the churn had been tampered with by some witch, like Mabel Martin's mother in Whittier's poem. Witches were sometimes supposed to work a baleful charm on the milk by putting under the doorsill some magical object, such as a picture of a toad or a lizard.

In Scotland, when churning was easy it was because of the secret help of the "brownie." He was a tiny, elf-like creature who lived in the barn and was never seen of men; but his presence was made known by his many deeds of helpfulness in kitchen and dairy, for which he was rewarded by a daily bowl of milk. Those who have read George MacDonald's story of Sir Gibbie remember how the little waif from the city was mistaken for a brownie because he secretly helped in the churning.

In France a pious class of peasants pray to St. Blaise for a blessing on their various farm occupations, including the dairy work. A hymn written to the saint contains this petition:—

> "In our dairies, curds and cream
> And fair cheeses may we see:
> Great St. Blaise, oh, grant our plea."[1]

Some such prayer as this may be running through the mind of the woman in our picture. She has the earnest and simple character which belongs to the Norman peasant. Hers is a kindly nature, too, and the cat rubs familiarly against her as if sure of a friend who has often set a saucer of milk in his way. With sleeves rolled up and skirts tucked about her, she attacks her work in a strong, capable way which shows that it is a pleasure. The light comes from some high window at the left, and, gleaming on her arms, shows how firm and hard the flesh is.

We know that this is a Norman peasant woman from her tall cap. There are many styles of caps peculiar to different parts of France, but those worn in Normandy are remarkable for their height. When some of the people of this province emigrated to the western continent and settled in Acadia, the land of Evangeline, the women brought their caps with them and continued to wear them many years, as we read in Longfellow's "Evangeline."

Our previous studies of the other pictures of this collection help us to see at once the good points of composition in the Woman Churning. The main lines of the group in the foreground form a tall pyramid. The shape of the churn gives us the line at the right side, and the figure of the cat carries the line of the woman's skirt into a corresponding slant on the left. The lines of the tiled floor add to the pyramidal effect by converging in perspective. Even the broom leaning against the shelf near the door takes the same diagonal direction as the tiles of the right side.

We have here also a new illustration of the art of treating inclosed spaces.[2] An outlet is given to the room through the door opening into the farmyard. Across the yard stands a low cow-shed, in which a woman is seated milking a cow. This building, however, does not altogether block up the view from the dairy door. Above the roof is a strip of sky, and through a square window at the back is seen a bit of the meadow.

[1]

From Ronsard's "Hymn to St. Blaise," translated by Henry Naegely in *J.F. Millet and Rustic Art.*

[2]

See chapters ii. and vi.

XV

THE MAN WITH THE HOE

To the peasant farmer every month of the year brings its own labors. From seed time to harvest there is a constant succession of different tasks, and hardly is the harvest gathered in before it is time to prepare again for planting. Before ploughing can be begun the fields must first be cleared of stubble and weeds. Now in Millet's village of Barbizon, this clearing of the fields was done, in his day, by means of an implement called in French a *houe*. Although we translate the word as hoe, the tool is quite unlike the American article of that name. It looks a little like a carpenter's adze, though much larger and heavier, the blade being as broad as that of a shovel. The handle is short and the implement is very clumsy and fatiguing to use. Even the stoutest peasant finds the work wearisome.

The man in our picture has paused for a moment's rest in this toilsome labor, and leans panting on his hoe. In the heat of his toil he has thrown off his hat and blouse, which now lie together on the ground behind him. His damp hair is matted together on his forehead, his brawny chest is exposed by the open shirt, his horny hands are clasped over the hoe handle. Some distant object catches his eye. It may be a farm wagon moving across the plain, or perhaps a bird flying through the clear air. To follow the course of such an object a moment is a welcome change from the monotonous rise and fall of the hoe.

It is a rough and uneven field in which the laborer works, rising here and there in small hillocks, and thickly overgrown with brambles and coarse tufts of herbage. When these weeds are loosened from the soil, they are raked in little heaps and burned. In the field just back of this is a circle of these bonfires, sending up their columns of smoke towards the sky. A young woman is busy raking together the piles. In the distance she looks like a priestess of ancient times presiding at some mystic rites of fire worship. Far beyond, a shapely tree is outlined against the horizon.

To study this picture profitably, we must consider separately the subject and the artistic qualities. These two elements in a work of art are often confused, but are in reality quite distinct. Very unpleasant subjects have sometimes been employed in pictures of great artistic merit, and again beautiful subjects have sometimes been treated very indifferently. When great art is united with a great subject, we have ideal perfection; but poor art and a poor subject together are intolerable. Now some people think only of the subject when they look at a picture, and others, more critical, look only at the qualities of art it contains. The best way of all is to try to understand something of both.

In the first glance at this picture we do not find the subject very attractive. The laborer is awkward, he is stupid looking, and he is very weary. If we are to look at laborers, we like to see them graceful, intelligent, and active like the Sower. As a redeeming quality, the Man with the Hoe has a certain patient dignity which commands our respect, but with all that, we do not call it a pleasant subject.

But look a moment at the strong, noble outlines of the drawing and see how finely modelled is the figure. So carefully did Millet study this work that he first modelled the figure in clay that he might give it more vitality in the painting. This Man with the Hoe seems indeed not a painted figure, but a real living, breathing human being, whom we can touch and find of solid flesh and blood.

We must note, too, how grandly the figure is thrown out against the sky and the plain. There is something to observe, also, in the proportions of the man to the background. The broad pyramid made by the bending figure and the hoe needs plenty of space at each side to set it off, hence the oblong shape of the picture. These, and other artistic qualities not so easily observed and understood, all give the picture "a place among the greater artistic conceptions of all time."

The Man with the Hoe has probably caused more discussion than any other of Millet's paintings. From the very first those who care only for the subject of a picture have condemned it, while the critics have praised its artistic qualities. Many have thought that Millet made the subject as unpleasant as possible in order to show the degrading effects of work. The same theory was suggested when the Sower and the Gleaners appeared. The painter himself was much troubled by these misunderstandings. "I have never dreamed of being a pleader in any cause," he said. He simply painted life as he saw it, and had no thought of teaching strange doctrines against labor. Indeed, no man ever felt more deeply than he the dignity of labor.

When everything which could be said for or against the picture had been exhausted on the other side of the Atlantic, the picture was brought to this country and finally to the State of California. Here the discussion began all over again. There were those who were so impressed by the unpleasant character of the subject that they could not find words strong enough to express their horror. The Man with the Hoe was called "a monstrous thing distorted and soul-quenched," a "dread" and "terrible" shape, "a thing that grieves not and that never hopes," a "brother to the ox," and many other things which would have surprised and grieved Millet.

Of course, any one to whom the pathos of the subject itself appeals so strongly can have little thought for the artistic qualities of the picture. So Edwin Markham, the writer of the poem from which these expressions are quoted, lets the subject lead him on into an impassioned protest against "the degradation of labor,—the oppression of man by man,"—all of which has nothing to do with the picture.

Millet was not one to care at all for what he called "pretty" subjects, as we have already seen in studying the picture of the Milkmaid. "He felt that only by giving to his figures the expression and character which belonged to their condition could he obey the laws of beauty in art, for he knew that a work of art is beautiful only when it is homogeneous."[1]

This was the theory which he put into practice in the Man with the Hoe, and one who understands well both his theories and his art sums up the great painting in these words: "The noble proportions of the figure alone would give this work a place among the greater artistic conceptions of all time, while the severe and simple pathos of this moment of respite in the interminable earth struggle, invests it with a sublimity which belongs to eternal things alone." [2]

[1]

Pierre Millet in the *Century*.

[2]

Henry Naegely.

XVI

THE PORTRAIT OF MILLET

In studying the works of any great painter many questions naturally arise as to the personality of the man himself and the influences which shaped his life. Some such questions have already been answered as we have examined these fifteen pictures by Millet. Jean François Millet, we have learned, was of peasant parentage and spent the greater part of his life in the country. His pious Norman ancestors bequeathed him a rich heritage of strong and serious traits. From them, too, he drew that patience and perseverance which helped him to overcome so many obstacles in his career.

In the surroundings of his childhood he saw no pictures and heard nothing of art or artists. Yet at a very early age he showed a remarkable talent for drawing. His artistic temperament was inherited from his father, who was a great lover of music and of everything beautiful. "Look," he sometimes said, plucking a blade of grass and showing it to his little boy, "how beautiful this is." His grandmother, too, had a true poetic vein in her nature. She would come to the child's bedside in the morning, calling, "Wake up, my little François, you don't know how long the birds have been singing the glory of God." In such a family the youth's gifts were readily recognized, and he was sent to Cherbourg, the nearest large town, to learn to be a painter. Here, and later in Paris, he received instruction from various artists, but his greatest teacher was Nature. So he turned from the schools of Paris, and the artificial standards of his fellow artists there, to study for himself, at first hand, the peasant life he wished to portray. What a delightful place Barbizon was for such work we have seen from some of his pictures.

It was during the fruitful years of work at Barbizon that Millet made the crayon portrait of himself which is reproduced as our frontispiece. He was a large, strong, deep-chested man, somewhat above the medium height. An admirer has described him as "one of nature's noblemen," and his younger brother Pierre says he was "built like a Hercules." He had an inherent distaste for fine clothes which he showed even in boyhood. When he grew to be a painter, and returned to visit his family in Gréville, the villagers were scandalized to see the city artist appear in their streets in blouse and sabots.

As we see in the portrait, Millet had long wavy hair, falling over his shoulders, and a thick black beard. His forehead was high and intelligent, and his nose delicately cut and sensitive. His eyes were gray-blue, of the kind which look a man through and through and which nothing escapes. The artist had so trained these wonderful eyes of his that he had only to turn them on a scene to photograph the impression indelibly on his memory.

The face that we see in the portrait is that of a thinker, a poet, and an artist. It is the face of one who held intimate converse with the great poets of the ages, of one whose favorite books were the Bible, Virgil, Theocritus and Shakespeare. Though Millet had many genial traits in his nature, his expression here is profoundly serious. Such an expression tells much of the inner life of the man. His pictures were too original to be popular at once, and while he waited for purchasers he found it hard to support his family. His anxieties wore upon his health, and he was subject to frequent headaches of frightful severity. Nor was the struggle with poverty his only trial. He had to contend constantly against the misconceptions and misrepresentations of hostile critics.

He was of too stern a nature and too loyal to his ideals to vary a hair's breadth from his course, yet criticism embittered him. "Give me signboards to paint, if you will," he exclaimed, "but at least let me think out my subjects in my own fashion and finish the work that I have to do, in peace."

Like all who have great originality, Millet lived in a world of his own, and had but a few congenial friends. To such friends, however, and in the inner circle of his home, he opened his great and tender heart, and all who knew him loved him.